The

The Prophet/ Honor Connection

ISBN 978-0-692-19034-0

Published by Chris Cody Ministries, Paducah, Kentucky
Printed in The U.S.A. by InstantPublisher.com

Book Design: David Hedrich

Cover Design: Melissa Kellenberger

Printed in the United States of America.
12345

Dedication

I'd like to dedicate this book to three men who have stood at the forefront of the prophet's ministry. These men have had a profound impact on the Body of Christ at large, and on my life individually.

Rev. Kenneth E. Hagin, Dr. Ed Dufresne, and Dr. Michael Jacobs, are men who have honorably served the Body of Christ and the world. Through their faithful example we better understand what it means to minister as a prophet. To each of you, I will be eternally grateful!

A Special thanks to my team of editors, graphic designers, and all Chris Cody Ministry partners for their vital contributions which made this project a reality.

I would also like to especially thank Dr. Michael Jacobs for his encouragement to get this revelation in print and out to the Body of Christ, as well as his generous financial support.

Formatting:
David Hedrich

Editors:
Dr. Suzanne Schultz
Ms. Tamara Lawson
Rev. Brett Barriger

Cover Design:
Melissa Kellenberger

Table of Contents

Foreword

I appreciate and value this revelation that God has given Dr. Cody on the subject of honor. Though I knew a little about honor, in many ways, Dr. Cody has opened a brand new revelation for all of us to explore. There is a law of faith and love, but I am seeing that there is a law that functions with honor towards people. The casual culture of today seems to demean honor.

If we gain the revelation of honor in our relationship with God, His Word, and with people, those relationships will be elevated. I highly recommend this message on honor that Dr. Cody has written. It will elevate your thinking toward everything you do.

Dr. Michael Jacobs

Introduction

In 2017, the Spirit of God began to reveal to me the link between the prophet's ministry and honor. Since that time, God has revealed to me more insights into this vital office of ministry, and the role honor plays in one's ability to receive from the anointing on a prophet.

It is my sincere and humble desire for each member of the Body of Christ to recognize the rare and precious *gift* Jesus gave to His church when He ascended on high and gave to some the ministry gift of the prophet. Only then will we receive all that our Lord intended we receive when He gave this bountiful gift. Honor is one way we unwrap the gift Jesus gave us in the prophet.

May this little book both inform and enlighten. Many blessings.

Dr. Chris Cody

Chapter 1
What is Honor?

Psalm 26:8 (KJV)

"LORD, I have loved the habitation of thy house, and the place where thine honor dwelleth."

I'd be remiss to teach you what God has revealed to me about the Prophet/Honor Connection without at least introducing you to the subject of honor itself.

Noah Webster defines "to honor" this way, **"To revere; to respect; to treat with deference and submission, and perform relative duties to."**[1] In grammatical terms, honor is a verb. It's something you do, something you show.

The Hebrew word translated honor means **weighty, or to make heavy**. In addition it carries the idea of *placing a high value on, to promote, to glorify, to dignify, to distinguish someone or something with excellence*.[2]

True honor is when you properly recognize someone or something to be rare and precious and to treat that someone or something accordingly. Conversely, to dishonor would be to handle something that should be treated as weighty, rare, and precious, with an attitude of lightness and casualness.

For instance, recently my wife pulled out our fine china for a family dinner. As we took our plates to get our food, I noticed two of my children holding their plates casually

---

[1] (Webster)

[2] (Strong)

with one hand. I corrected them and told them to be careful, to handle that plate with care, and to hold it securely with two hands. Why? Because those dishes are rare and precious to us. They are very expensive, hard to replace, and are very sentimental to Amber and I because they were given to us as wedding gifts. I've never had that kind of thought when we carried paper plates to dinner! Obviously, paper plates don't deserve the honor that fine china does.

I wonder how you're treating spiritual things. Do you treat them like fine china or like disposable paper plates? "Casual" has become a buzzword in today's culture, and we in the Body of Christ must be very careful to not let the world's embrace of all things casual to creep into our mindset towards God and holy things.

I have been greatly criticized for my unbending stand on my approach to how I "do church". Many pastors today get up in the same clothes they might wear to go get a slurpy at 7-11. I don't and never will. I endeavor to create a welcoming, inviting environment, while preserving the great sanctity and dignity that our coming together to worship God deserves. I endeavor to bring my honor to church, and to the people I minister to, because I recognize the high value God places on people, on His Word, and on His House.

As we will see in the next chapter, *honor is a foundational issue*. If your foundation is faulty or in disrepair, what you build on that foundation is subject to calamity and destruction. It's my aim to build my life on a solid foundation so that my life will count and my ministry will endure. We will see that honor is a key ingredient to drawing out of the prophet's mantle all that God has for us through that ministry office, but don't forget that honor is an important ingredient to success in all our relationships, both with God and men.

Chapter 2:
Honor: A Foundational Issue

Honor is a one of God's core values. It is not only a foundational issue, it's also a spiritual law. Get honor right and you can go far in God and in life. Get honor wrong, and you will forfeit much. I often encourage those who will listen to make me a promise to become lifelong students of the subject of honor.

The law of honor is stated in 1 Samuel chapter two.

1 Samuel 2:30b (GW)
30b "But now the LORD declares: I promise that *I will honor those who honor me, and those who despise me will be considered insignificant.* [3]

God honors those who honor Him. Those who dishonor, demean, and lightly esteem God, His Word, and His things, will in turn be treated by Him in the same way. The High Priest Eli, and his two sons Hophni and Phineas, had a place of honor in the service of God, but they lost it, and their lives, because of their dishonor.

Though thousands of years have passed since God revealed the law of honor, He has not changed His mind about the subject. I'm going to say it again, honor is a foundational issue in our lives.

The first commandment with promise is a commandment to honor. "Honor thy father and mother: that thy days may

---

[3] God's Word Translation

be long upon the land which the Lord thy God giveth thee." **Exodus 20: 12** Husbands and wives are instructed to honor each other **(1 Peter. 3: 7; Eph. 5: 11)**. We are commanded to honor authorities and political leaders. **(Rom. 13: 1-7)** Employees are commanded to honor their employers. **(1 Tim. 6: 1)** Believers are encouraged to honor those who have spiritual authority and oversight over their lives. **(Heb. 13: 17)** The Bible declares that the house of God, the local church, is to be a place where "honor dwells". **(Psalm 26: 8)** Paul tells Timothy that we are to strive to become vessels of honor, able and fit for the Master's use. In other words, you and I determine both HOW and TO WHAT DEGREE God can use us. It is our job to become vessels of honor and to separate ourselves from all things that defile and contaminate. **(2 Tim. 2: 20-21)**

These verses serve to illustrate the high place honor is to hold in every Christian's daily life. Honor is to touch and up gird every major relationship we have in this life, whether it's our relationship with God, with our pastor or spiritual father, our spouse, our kids, our employers, and so forth.

Much could and needs to be said about the subject of honor. The failure to honor is costing this generation much, and before there can be a full restoration of the power of God, the presence of God, and the full demonstration of the gifts of the Spirit in our midst, there must be a restoration of honor in the church.

The rest of this book will focus on the unique connection between the ministry of the prophet and honor, but make no mistake, honor is a foundational issue that will impact every key relationship you and I have, not just the prophet's ministry.

Would you make me a promise? Promise me that from this day forward you will become a lifelong student of the subject of honor. God will reward you richly if you do!

Chapter 3

The Prophet's Office

Ephesians 4:11-12 (KJV) Emphasis Added

[11] *And he (Jesus) gave some, apostles; and some, prophets; and some, evangelists; and some, pastors and teachers;* [12] *For the perfecting of the saints, for the work of the ministry, for the edifying of the body of Christ.)*[4]

1 Corinthians 12:28 (NKJV) Emphasis Added

[28] *And God has appointed these in the church: first apostles, second prophets, third teachers, after that miracles, then gifts of healings, helps, administrations, varieties of tongues.* [5]

There is a legitimate, necessary, ministry of the prophet in the church today. You may not have recognized it but there is. You may have been turned off by the extremism and excess of others who have claimed to be a prophet and weren't, but there still is a true prophet in the earth today. **We need to learn to recognize that office of ministry and how to receive from it!**

The five ministry offices are each different in their operation, anointing, and function, yet they all have the very same overall objective. "Jesus gave..." (Eph. 4: 11) and "God appointed" (1 Cor. 12: 28) each of these offices of ministry in the church for the purpose of:

> ➢ The perfecting of the saints for the work of the ministry.
> ➢ The building up of the Body of Christ.

---

4 (Thomas Nelson Publishers)
5 (Holman Bible Publishers)

18

> Causing believers to grow and mature into the full measure of the stature of Christ.

A true prophet has a part in this, just like the pastor and the teacher does. The prophet's ministry is a wonderful ministry, one of great responsibility, one which will bless your spiritual life tremendously, if you will learn to recognize and receive from that office and anointing.

To those who say, "There are no apostles or prophets in the church today," I respectfully say, "Give me scripture!" I can't find any scripture in the New Testament that nullifies the ministry of the apostle or prophet. I wonder about the arrogance of people who dare to remove from the church offices of ministry that were SET there by the Lord, Jesus Christ, and have no Scriptural support for their declaration!

We rob the Body of Christ of rich blessing when we negate these two important offices of ministry. They are there for our equipping, maturing, and upbuilding. How are people going to ever recognize the true ministry of the prophet when preachers keep insisting there aren't any!

I look back on my development as a Christian, and I can see the dramatic influence the prophet's office has had in my life. I was introduced to Rev. Kenneth E. Hagin's ministry in the mid 1990's. He stood in the forefront of the prophet's ministry during that time. Then, God divinely connected me to another prophet of God, Dr. Ed Dufresne in 2004. He spoke into my life as my spiritual father until he went to heaven in 2013. Now, another prophet of God, Dr. Michael Jacobs is speaking into my life.

Time would fail me to tell of all the wonderful ways my life and ministry have been transformed through these men's prophetic ministry. I wouldn't be who I am today, or have the anointing I have today, or have the revelation of the

Word I walk in today, if it wasn't in great part to the prophet's ministry. So, you can understand I have a great interest, though my ministry is that of the pastor and the teacher, in the prophet's ministry.

God has something for you too through the prophet's mantle, for it is a ministry office listed among four others that Jesus gave unto men for the perfecting of the saints that they might do their part in the work of the ministry!

The following is a brief summary of the characteristics of the true New Testament prophet's ministry:

> ➢ Prophets are first and foremost preachers and teachers of the Word of God. They have places to preach. They are full time ministers. There are no prophets among the laity. I like to say it this way, there are no prophets working at Walmart. Prophets are seasoned ministers who have been in the ministry for many years. They came up through the ranks of the lower offices of the evangelist, pastor, or teacher, and after being proven faithful were brought into the higher office of the prophet. (Ephesians 4: 11; 1 Corinthians 12: 28)

> ➢ Prophets are ministers who have visions and or revelations. (Zech. 12:1) They are seers. To constitute the office of the prophet, one must have consistent manifestations of two out of the three revelation gifts: the word of knowledge, the word of wisdom, the discerning of spirits, plus prophecy.

> ➢ Prophets speak for God. (Jer. 1:9) They have unique insight into the mind and heart of God. They are made to feel what God feels. Their ministry is not local, they are called to the whole body of Christ.

20

➢ Prophets speak by inspiration of the moment. Their words carry great weight, for God will not allow the words of His prophets to fall to the ground. (1 Sam. 3:19)

The following are important distinctions between Old Testament prophets and New Testament Prophets:

➢ In the Old Testament, the prophet was the only preacher they had. The only other office that carried an anointing back then was the prophet, the priest, and the king.

➢ In the Old Testament, people inquired of God through a prophet. God would give individuals, and the nation of Israel as a whole, guidance and direction through the prophet.

This is very important! In the New Testament, every child of God has been born again, born of the Spirit of God, and are to be personally led by the Spirit of God. Therefore, it is unscriptural in the New Covenant to inquire of a prophet for direction and guidance.

➢ New Testament prophets do at times foretell future events, but that's not the primary emphasis of the New Testament prophet, as it was under the Old Testament. They do more "forth-telling" (speaking by inspiration of the Spirit at the moment) than "fore-telling" (predicting future events).

I trust that the Holy Spirit will enable you to recognize this office of ministry and teach you how to benefit from all that Jesus put in the prophet to aid and bless your life! May this little book assist you in that endeavor.

Chapter 4

The Prophet/Honor Connection

Please read this passage prayerfully and thoughtfully. It is of profound importance to the subject at hand.

Mark 6:1-6 (NKJV)

1 Then He went out from there and came to His own country, and His disciples followed Him. 2 And when the Sabbath had come, He began to teach in the synagogue. And many hearing Him were astonished, saying, "Where did this Man get these things? And what wisdom is this which is given to Him, that such mighty works are performed by His hands! 3 Is this not the carpenter, the Son of Mary, and brother of James, Joses, Judas, and Simon? And are not His sisters here with us?" ***And they were offended at Him****. 4 But Jesus said to them, "****A prophet is not without honor*** *except in his own country, among his own relatives, and in his own house." 5* ***Now He could do no mighty work there****, except that He laid His hands on a few sick people and healed them. 6 And* ***He marveled because of their unbelief****. Then He went about the villages in a circuit, teaching.*[6]

Marvelous, supernatural things happened during the ministry of the Lord Jesus Christ when He walked this earth. Jesus performed miracles that had never been recorded before by any other prophet that came before Him. Jesus accomplished miraculous works that *"none other man did"* (John 15: 24), proving everywhere He went that He was the Anointed One, the Prophet that was to come, like unto Moses, the One Israel was commanded to hear.

---

[6] (Holman Bible Publishers)

Acts 7:37 (KJV)
37 This is that Moses, which said unto the children of Israel, A
prophet shall the Lord your God raise up unto you of your
brethren, like unto me; him shall ye hear.[7]

This Prophet of God had been traveling the region of Galilee preaching the gospel of the Kingdom of God and performing supernatural acts. Mark chapter five gives an account of a day in the life and ministry of Jesus. He came into the country of the Gadarenes. There, Jesus set free the madman of Gadara from demonic possession, healed the woman with the issue of blood, and raised a young girl from the dead…not a bad day of ministry!

Unfortunately, Mark chapter six reads quite differently than Mark chapter five. When Jesus came to his hometown of Nazareth, He was not able to produce the same miraculous results. I know, I know what you're thinking, "How could you say that Jesus was not able!" But that's exactly what the Bible says. Jesus COULD THERE DO NO MIGHTY WORK (Mark 6: 5). **It didn't say He *would* not, it said He *could* not.**

Why was Jesus unable to perform the signs, wonders, and mighty deeds that He performed everywhere else? Because **the people of Nazareth did not understand the prophet/honor connection.**

"a *prophet* is not *without honor*…" Mark 6:4

There is a prophet/honor connection.

There were people in Nazareth that needed to be healed, who could have been healed, but they weren't. No doubt there were people present that Jesus wanted to deliver and

---

7 (Thomas Nelson Publishers)

set free from satanic power and bondage, but they were not. Why? It wasn't because Jesus wasn't willing. It was because the people failed to honor, and that failure to honor disqualified them from receiving what Jesus had in Him to give. I want you to see that honor qualifies one to receive. Dishonor disqualifies.

Honor connects you to the prophet's anointing. There is something about honor that makes a demand on the prophets mantle and causes the ministry of the prophet to operate. *People who fail to honor can never receive from God's minister what those who honor will.*

Luke records that Jesus entered the synagogue in Nazareth, as His habit was, and stood up to read. He found the place in the Book of Isaiah where it said, "The Spirit of the Lord is upon Me, because He hath anointed me to preach the gospel to the poor; he hath sent me to heal the brokenhearted, to preach deliverance to the captives, and recovering of sight to the blind, to set at liberty them that are bruised, to preach the acceptable year of the Lord." Then He declared, "This day this Scripture is fulfilled in your hearing. (Luke 4: 18-21)

Jesus wasn't boasting in this declaration. He was informing. He was letting the people of Nazareth know what He was anointed to do, so they could in turn respond to that anointing in faith and receive their needs met by receiving from His anointing. Instead, they reduced Jesus. They failed to recognize Him for who He truly was.

A KEY TO HONOR

A key to honor is recognition. *You cannot receive from an anointing you don't recognize.* Believers need to be trained to recognize, reverence, and receive from the anointing on men. Failure to recognize the anointing on God's servants is a form of dishonor, and you can see from this account in Mark and Luke that it disqualified them from receiving from the prophets mantle.

You understand why I keep referring to Jesus as a prophet right? I fully understand that Jesus is the Son of God, the long-promised Messiah, our Redeemer. I am not diminishing Jesus' place, or His ministry by calling Him a prophet, for He was a prophet.

In truth, Jesus came to the people of Nazareth, intending to minister to them out of the prophets anointing on His life. How do I know this? Because when the people of Nazareth became offended at Him, Jesus' first response was, "*A prophet* is not without honor..." That tells me that He came to them as a prophet. It also tells me that it was their lack of honor that hindered Jesus' ministry in Nazareth.

"But Pastor Chris it also says that they were offended at Him and that Jesus marveled at their unbelief. What about that?" Great question. The offense and the unbelief are simply the fruit of the evil root of dishonor. Had they honored, they would not have been offended. Had they honored, they would not have fallen into unbelief. See, here we are again. Honor is a foundational issue.

The Danger of Becoming Familiar

Let's examine Jesus' statement about the prophet's ministry and honor more closely.

Mark 6:2-5 (Passion NT)

Afterward, Jesus left Capernaum and returned with his disciples to Nazareth, his hometown. On the Sabbath, he went to teach in the synagogue. Everyone who heard his teaching was overwhelmed with astonishment. They said among themselves, "What incredible wisdom has been given to him! Where did he receive such profound insights? And what mighty miracles flow through his hands! Isn't this Mary's son, the carpenter, the brother of Jacob, Joseph, Judah, and Simon? And don't his sisters all live here in Nazareth?" And they took offense at him. Jesus said to them, "A prophet is treated with honor everywhere except in his own hometown, among his relatives, and in his own house." ⁵ He was unable to do any great miracle in Nazareth, except to heal a few sick people by laying his hands upon them. He was amazed at the depth of their unbelief!

You can readily see the thing that caused the people of Nazareth to get tripped up. They failed to honor because of familiarity. Where is a prophet without honor? In his own hometown, among his own relatives, in his own house. Why would that be? Familiarity! They had grown so accustomed to the humanity of Jesus that they failed to recognize Him as the Anointed One. They were blinded to the greatness of Jesus. They failed to receive from the Prophet that day because they reduced Jesus down to nothing more than the little boy they knew all those years ago, the son of Joseph, the son of a carpenter.

They only knew Jesus after the flesh. They failed to know Him after the Spirit.

It's an awesome privilege to be close to the man of God, but with that privilege there is a great danger that we must be aware of and always guard against, and that is the danger of becoming familiar. The one that we once held in such high esteem can become "common" over time. The longer we are around someone we begin to see their humanity, their natural side, and if we're not careful we begin to think, "Hey, they're just like me!" We begin to reduce them in our thinking, and when we do, we can lose our sense of value and honor for the anointing and office that person carries.

I never let myself become familiar with my spiritual father. We aren't pals. I am not his equal in the ministry. He is the father, and I the son. He is the teacher, and I the student. I am always careful to separate the man from the mantle, but I love and honor both.

That's why Jesus said, "a prophet is not without honor except in his own hometown, among his own relatives, and in his own house." It saddens me that the honor for the pastor's office has been removed from the modern church. Instead of pastor, he's a life coach. Instead of pastor, it's just Chris. When people do that to me, I know they've lost the honor for my office. I've noticed that once familiarity sets in, that person never receives from my ministry the same way again.

When you don't *perceive*, you fail to *receive*. Stated another way, you receive on the level you perceive, and this is vital to the prophet/honor connection.

Matthew 10:41-42 (NKJV) Emphasis Added

*41 He who **receives a prophet in the name of a prophet shall receive a prophet's reward**. And he who **receives a righteous man** in the name of a righteous man shall receive a righteous man's reward. 42 And whoever gives one of these little ones only a cup of cold water **in the name of a disciple**, assuredly, I say to you, he shall by no means lose his reward."*[8]

Have you ever considered that Jesus was not referring to three different people in these verses, but instead that He is referring to a prophet who is received differently by different people? Some received him as a prophet, and were

---

[8] (Holman Bible Publishers)

rewarded on that level. Some received him as a righteous man, and they were rewarded on that level. Then others received him as a disciple, and they were rewarded accordingly.

Notice also the descending order of how this prophet was being received, being reduced to lower levels each time. prophet, righteous man, disciple. *The Spirit of God pointed out to me the fact that because the people of Nazareth didn't receive Jesus as a prophet that it forced Jesus to descend into the lower office of the teacher. "*...then He went about their villages in a circuit teaching." (Mark 6:6)

Teaching is wonderful, but it was far less than what they could have received had they recognized and received Jesus as a prophet!

Your reward is determined by your recognition. There is a prophet/honor connection!

RECEIVING A PROPHET

The prophet's office must be received for his ministry to be effective and fruitful. It's amazing to me how some think they can receive from God while dishonoring the very one God sent to minister to them.

In the church I pastor, we are very blessed to have wonderful, seasoned ministers come to minister and impart to our congregation every year. Some stand in the office of the prophet. We continue to receive revelation into the plan of God, impartations that equip and further us in our callings, and people are healed and delivered.

Every passing year, we continue to see greater and greater things, and one of the reasons for this is the way we "receive" the minister. We have learned that the more we do to welcome, pray for, and honor the guest minister, the more we receive from their ministry. We strive to do all we can to assist that minister in getting into the fullness of their office and anointing.

Romans 15:29 (NKJV) Emphasis Added

[29] *But I know that when I come to you, **I shall come in the fullness of the blessing** of the gospel of Christ.*[9]

When our man of God comes, we want him to come in the fullness of that office! We've learned that it's not just up to the minister to have a fruitful meeting, but that the receiver has a part to play as well. So, we honor that man or woman of God.

We don't treat them casually. We highly esteem them, for we know how rare and precious it is to be able to receive from that gift and anointing. We put them in the best hotel our city has to offer. We do all we can to make sure they have time to rest, pray, and be refreshed before each service. We do what we can to find out what kind of music helps the minister and what kind hinders them. Do they like to sing long, or short? Do they like to chat before service, or do they like to be quiet and pray in the Holy Ghost? Whatever it is, we just flow.

Pastors, train your people how to receive from the prophet's ministry. Prophets are different. They aren't straight teachers. They minister differently. Teach your people what's available in the prophet's mantle that's not available in your pastoral ministry. That's what Jesus was doing in Luke 4: 18. He told the people what He was anointed to do, not to boast, but because He wanted the

---

[9] (Holman Bible Publishers)

people to know what was available to them through that anointing that was on His life!

If pastors don't teach and train their people, they won't be able to receive on the level they need to, and God will hold us responsible. Many think all that prophets do is prophesy, and if the minister doesn't give half the congregation "a word" they'll think the prophet was "off his game" or something. We have to study the ministry of the prophet and teach our people the different ways God uses them beyond just prophecy. That way, we become skillful in receiving what God wants us to receive!

If the congregation just receives them as a guest speaker, then they won't receive the prophet's reward. They'll receive the guest speaker's reward! Matthew 10: 41 We make it a point before the prophet of God comes to town to let all of heaven know that we receive them as a gift from God and as a prophet! I often find myself praying, "Father, let there be a room made ready, fully furnished and prepared that the prophet can simply step into and minister to us!" Praise God!

Receiving and honoring is not about hero worship, and it's certainly not about buying anything. It is recognizing that there is a connection between showing proper honor and receiving from the ministry of the prophet! We've discovered it and we are reaping the rich results of it!

This encounter between Jesus and the people of Nazareth highlight for us the high price of dishonor. The dishonor that is so prevalent in the world has infected the church, and it is costing us much. Many are hungry for revival and they long to experience God's holy presence, His glory, and to see His power made manifest in the earth. I believe they are sincere, and I share in their desire. We must come to terms; however, that the church will never experience what she seeks until both the preachers and the people restore the honor!

When we begin to see true honor for God, His ministers, His church, and His word restored, we can know of assurance that the rain of God's power is soon to fall!

Chapter 5

Honor Must Be Repaid

Let's look at an Old Testament example of the prophet/honor connection at work. In 2 Kings Chapter 4 there is an account given of a Shunamite woman's interaction with the prophet Elisha.

2 Kings 4:8-17 (KJV)

8 And it fell on a day, that Elisha passed to Shunem, where was a great woman; and she constrained him to eat bread. And so it was, that as oft as he passed by, he turned in thither to eat bread. 9 And she said unto her husband, <u>Behold now, I perceive that this is an holy man of God, which passeth by us continually. 10 Let us make a little chamber, I pray thee, on the wall; and let us set for him there a bed, and a table, and a stool, and a candlestick: and it shall be, when he cometh to us, that he shall turn in thither</u>. 11 And it fell on a day, that he came thither, and he turned into the chamber, and lay there. 12 And he said to Gehazi his servant, Call this Shunammite. And when he had called her, she stood before him.13 And he said unto him, Say now unto her, Behold, thou hast been careful for us with all this care; what is to be done for thee? wouldest thou be spoken for to the king, or to the captain of the host? And she answered, I dwell among mine own people. 14 And he said, What then is to be done for her? And Gehazi answered, Verily she hath no child, and her husband is old. 15 And he said, Call her. And when he had called her, she stood in the door. 16 And he said, About this season, according to the time of life, thou shalt embrace a son. And she said, Nay, my lord, thou man of God, do not lie unto thine *handmaid.* [17] *And the woman conceived, and bare a son at that season that Elisha had said unto her, according to the time of life.*[10]

The transformation of one's whole life is often initiated by the seeming smallest of encounters. The woman from Samaria that encountered Jesus while performing a daily, routine task at the well comes to mind. That single encounter with the Master changed her whole life, and it all began with the recognition, "Sir, I perceive that Thou art a prophet..." John 4: 19.

In this passage, we see a woman from Shunem have such an encounter with the foremost prophet of her day. Many had to have seen the passerby Elisha coming and going, but this particular woman recognized something different about this man. She said to her husband, "Behold now, I PERCEIVE THAT THIS IS A HOLY MAN OF GOD...".

She perceived! It is the first step in receiving from the anointing on any minister, but then notice that her *perception* affected her *reception*. Her proper perception invoked within her the desire to honor. When you're an honorable person, you're just looking for an opportunity to be honorable.

With no other motivation but to honor and show love and care for the man of God, she turns to her husband and says, "Let us make *a little chamber, I pray thee, on the wall; and let us set for him there a bed, and a table, and a stool, and a candlestick, and it shall be, when he cometh to us, that he shall turn in thither.*"

The English text here is quite deceiving to the reader. The words chamber on the wall, and table, stool, and candlestick, paint the picture of something like an old cot on a side,

---

[10] (Thomas Nelson Publishers)

dimly lit room with an old wooden table and stool; but I did some study and discovered that the word chamber, *'Aliyah* in Hebrew, was a room many homes had in the East. Here is how Dr. Finis Dake describes such a room in his Bible commentary[11]

"`*Aliyah* generally refers to an upper room of an Eastern house, sometimes built on the roof or as a second story to the porch, accessed by stairs. It is called "the chamber over the gate" in 2Sam. 18:33. The chamber here is "on the wall," perhaps because a window opening to the street was the only evidence that a new room had been added. **Such a room was usually well furnished and kept for the entertainment of honored guests. Such a room made a desirable place of retirement for the master of the house**...It was in an `aliyah that Daniel prayed daily in the midst of idolatry (Dan. 6:10). In the N.T. it **is called an upper room** (Acts 1:13; 9:37,39; 20:7-8). **In such a place Christ ate the Passover with His disciples** (Mk. 14:15; Lk. 22:12)."

The word "stool" is also a misleading one for modern readers. Again, to quote Dake, "The Hebrew word translated stool here comes from a root word that means "to cover." **It refers to a canopied seat, or "throne" and is translated throne 127 times in the Bible. This was no doubt the best piece of furniture the rich woman could get for the prophet**."[12]

Now you have a more accurate picture of the extent to which this woman and her husband went to honor the one they perceived to be a man of God. Her level of reception and hospitality tells you something about her perception of

---

[11] (Dake) *Eastern Rooms Commentary Dake's Annotated Study Bible 2 Kings 4: 10)*

[12] (Dake) *Dake's Annotated Reference Bible: Containing the Old and New Testaments of the Authorized or King James Version Text.*

the man she was honoring. What she did and how she did it is a lesson for us all on what true honor is. She placed a high value on the prophet and cared for his comfort and wellbeing. She recognized something special about him and she treated him as a rare and precious gift.

MOTIVE MATTERS

For honor to be honor, one's motive must be pure. We are about to see the powerful, supernatural, blessings that result when we recognize and show proper honor to the man of God, but know of a surety that if your motive isn't pure, it isn't honor, and the reward won't be the same.

When you study this account of the Shunamite woman and her honor and care for the Prophet Elisha, you will see that she had pure motives. She never made a demand on him for anything. She never tried to gain some advantage in return for her honor and care, nor did she try to curry favor in return for her generosity. Her desire was to be a blessing! All she ever wanted was to be a supply to the man of God, and make his journey to and from a more restful, peaceful one.

HONOR MUST BE REPAID!

On her side, she honored, loved, and cared for God's servant, but now we must look at what such actions provoke in the heart of God and in His prophet. As I've said before, when you show honor you have triggered a spiritual law, and you may not have been in it for the reward, but that honor must be repaid, for the law of honor says, "for those who honor Me, I will honor..." 1 Sam. 2: 30

After many days, something stirred the heart of the prophet Elisha. As he lay resting in this chamber of honor, he said to his servant Gehazi, "Call this Shunamite." When she came to him he said, "You have been careful for us with all this care. The Amplified says, "you have been most painstaking and reverently concerned for us." **WHAT IS TO BE DONE FOR THEE?"**

See! Something must be done for the one who honors! Elisha goes on, "Would you be spoken for to the king?" "Would you like me to speak to the Captain of the Army?" Her heart and motive are revealed in her response, "And she answered, no I dwell among my own people." 2 Kings 4: 13 If I could paraphrase, she said, "No. I'm good. I just wanted to bless you!" So she left.

Yet, Elisha wouldn't let it go! He said again to his servant, "What then is to be done for her?" I read this once and God thundered in My spirit, "HONOR MUST BE REPAID!" It came as such a rich and powerful revelation to my heart! HONOR MUST BE REPAID. IT IS SPIRITUAL LAW.

Then, Gehazi got to the heart of it. He said, "Verily, she hath no child, and her husband is old." Elisha said, "Call her."

Oh child of God, I pray you get this truth! The woman was called, and so she came a second time, only this time the prophet of God declared, "About this season, according to the time of life, thou shalt embrace a son." 2 Kings 4: 16 **Her honor caused her unspoken, deepest, desire and longing of her heart, to be a mother, to be known and granted!**

She was taken aback. "Nay, my lord, thou man of God, do not lie unto thine handmaid!" 2 Kings 4: 17 Can I give you the Cody translation of that verse? She said, "Don't you do me like that man of God! I didn't ask you for anything, but you're messing with a momma's heart, don't get my hopes up like that!"

A year later, just as the prophet of God said, she embraced a son.

She perceived, received, and honored the prophet because he was a prophet, and for doing so, she received the prophet's reward.

Matthew 10:41 (KJV)
41 He that receiveth a prophet in the name of a prophet shall receive a prophet's reward.

What is the prophet's reward? It's the deepest desire and longing of your heart!

My wife and I have experienced the prophet's reward in our own lives. After pastoring our church for a few years, the word of the Lord came to me in a time of prayer saying, "I want you to relocate your ministry and get in position for a last day move of My Spirit." That endeavor took us seven difficult years of sacrifice to accomplish and one that is still being advanced to this day.

During these seven years, my wife and I knew that God had a nicer home for us, one that would more fully meet the desires of our heart and the needs of our growing family. Yet for years, we knew that it wasn't time and that we needed to continue to sacrifice, putting our finances towards fulfilling the assignment God gave us to relocate our ministry, and so we did.

Then, while sitting in a meeting where our spiritual father was ministering, he stopped preaching and pointed his finger at Amber and I. He said, "Why do I see a home, and lands, and a barn, and trees?" He went on to prophesy that God would bring us to the home He had for us and described what we had in our hearts exactly! In fact, the prophet of God went on to say, "Now I know what to do

40

with those two horses," he gave them to us! Little did he know that I had dreamed of having a horse since I was a boy, but had never had one.

My wife and I honored God, we honored the plan of God, we honored our spiritual father, and over time, that honor made a demand on the law of honor. HONOR MUST BE REPAID!

Our family lives in that home today and it's got land, and trees, and a barn, and horses! Through the ministry of the prophet and the flow of honor, the Cody's have experienced the prophet's reward!

Let me tell you about another instance in which our ministry was impacted by the prophet's ministry.

The Lord had led us to finance the major part of our church building's construction through a bond program. This is a financial product that has advantages over traditional lending but comes at a cost, typically a higher interest rate and payment.

Our goal, once having completed construction and gaining occupancy, was to refinance our bond loan to a more traditional financing product. This would save the ministry thousands of dollars a month.

In our bond program, our payment mushroomed higher and higher every year the first four years. Each time placing more pressure on our ministry financially. We diligently searched to find a new lender but to no avail…UNTIL THE PROPHET SPOKE!

During a series of meetings with Dr. Michael Jacobs, who stands in the ministry of the prophet, the Spirit of God came upon him, and he began to prophesy about our building and a new lender. These words came forth from the prophet's lips...

"I'm going to move in your life saith the Lord and help you with this building. I'm upgrading you and Pastor Amber today. New money is coming. New projects will be funded, some by the church, and some probably from an outside lender, and I'm working on that lender, saith the Lord..."

We had been praying, standing in faith, and speaking the promise of God as we pursued the lender, but within just a few months after receiving this prophecy, we had found that new lender, secured a better loan, including the paving of our parking lot, and best of all, saving our ministry almost $4,000 per month on the payment!

Since that time, the church has experienced the upgrade God promised through the prophet's words. Our bills have gone down and our income has gone up glory to God!

I thank God for the prophet! I thank God that we held those services! I'm so glad we honored the prophet's anointing!

BEING ONE OF THE FEW

It's not recorded that any other person in Shunem received any help or supernatural benefit from the prophet's mantle Elisha carried, only this woman and her family received. They all had a prophet in their midst, but that mantle didn't benefit any others because they didn't perceive who and what they had.

Like her, we have recognized and done our best to honor the gift God gave us in the prophet of God, and in doing so, our personal lives and ministry have been radically blessed.

The mantle of the prophet, not necessarily the man himself, is sensitive to the law of honor. On our side, our desire should be like the Shunamite woman's. We simply want to be a supply and to show our love and affection for the prophet's ministry, and the very special one who carries it. On God's side, He will continue to watch over His word to perform it, looking for those special people who perceive and then receive the gift of God. To them, their honor MUST BE REPAID!

Chapter 6

The Open Door of Honor

2 Kings 4: 17 (KJV)

"And the woman conceived, and bare a son at that season that Elisha had said unto her, according to the time of life."[13]

God is a faith God. He always has been, and He always will be. Apart from faith it is impossible to please Him. Faith is the currency of heaven. It is what we offer Him in order to receive what He has for us. "But without faith *it is* impossible to please *him*: for he that cometh to God must believe that he is, and *that* he is a rewarder of them that diligently seek him." Hebrews 11: 6 Yet, as important as faith is, it is not the only door through which one can receive from God.

How was God able to get this miracle to the Shunamite woman? It wasn't because of her faith. It is evident that she didn't have faith for children because she didn't have any. There is no record that she spent time, like Hannah did, calling upon God in prayer to grant her desire for a son. She wasn't praying for a son. She wasn't expecting one. By all accounts, she and her husband had resigned themselves to the reality that they had gone childless and now, he at least, was too old to have children.

It speaks volumes to me of how absent faith was in her heart for children in that when the prophet Elisha said, "What must be done for you?" that she never mentioned it!

---

[13] (Thomas Nelson Publishers)

She didn't even put in a prayer request! I get prayer requests all the time from people that I know are not in faith about the thing they are requesting prayer for, but at least they believed it possible enough to ask for us to pray about it!

So, how did a woman receive the miracle of being able to conceive and give birth to a son that she didn't have faith for? How did God get this miracle into this woman's life apart from faith? *He did it through the open door of honor*!

I'm not diminishing the importance of faith, and having faith. *I am* unapologetically though trying to elevate in your thinking the weight honor carries in the mind of God, and in heaven!

Her son was not the fruit of her faith. Her son was the reward for her honor.

Some blessings come by our faith. They manifest because we stepped out on the promise of God, believed it in our heart, spoke it with our mouth, and God's power brought it to pass! It's also equally true though that God is a God of reward! He is a rewarder!

Psalm 127:3 (KJV) Emphasis Added
3 Lo, children are an heritage of the LORD: and ***the fruit of the womb is his reward***.[14]

The fruit of the womb is his reward! God was able to bless the fruit of this woman's womb as a reward for the honor she showed His servant!

If there is a door through which God can reach my life with miracles, signs, wonders, and blessings, then bless God I want to do whatever I have to on my side to make sure that door stays open. I don't know about you, but I'm still

---

[14] (Thomas Nelson Publishers)

working on my faith. I'm striving every day to become more skillful with the faith God gave me, but I'm so glad to discover that God can still reach me through the open door of honor, even if my faith is undeveloped in some area.

God has put the ministry gifts in the Body of Christ for the perfecting and building up of the saints. Those precious ministry gifts, including that of the prophet, will enrich your life, beyond your faith, if you will be a person of honor.

Many people appealed to the Lord Jesus for aid who did not have faith during His earthly ministry. Yet all who appealed to Him from their hearts left their encounter with Jesus with their miracle. Even the Syrophoenician woman received deliverance for her daughter as she humbly, persistently appealed to the Master for help. Jesus schooled her into faith and got her talking out of her heart, and that was enough to get her daughter delivered! The Nobleman received deliverance for his son even though he didn't have faith, as he cried out to Jesus, "I believe, help thou mine unbelief." (Mark 7: 28; 9: 24)

By their seeking, their persistence, their recognition of Jesus as the One who could help them, they honored, even on a small level, and received their miracle through the open door of honor.

I remember an instance that was related to me about a woman who lay dying in her hospital room. She was young and had a husband and a few small children. Suddenly, she saw Jesus and immediately assumed that He had come to take her to heaven. She said, "Oh Jesus! I can't go to heaven yet, I have small children I need to raise!" She said that Jesus smiled at her sweetly and said, "Daughter, I've not come to take you to heaven. I've come to heal you. You're a tither!"

"What does being a tither have to do with healing?" you may ask. Well, tithing is showing honor to God!

Proverbs 3:9-10 (KJV) Emphasis Added
[9] *Honour the LORD with thy substance, and with the firstfruits of all thine increase:* [10] *So shall thy barns be filled with plenty, and thy presses shall burst out with new wine.*[15]

In Malachi, God says, "If I be a father, where is my honor?" "Bring ye all the tithes into the storehouse, that there may be meat in my house, and prove me now herewith, saith the Lord of hosts if I will not open you the windows of heaven, and pour you out a blessing that there be not room enough to receive. And I will rebuke the devourer for your sakes AND YOUR VINE WILL NOT CAST HER FRUIT BEFORE THE TIME IN THE FIELD, SAITH THE LORD OF HOSTS, and all nations SHALL CALL YOU BLESSED: for ye shall be a delightsome land, saith the Lord of hosts." Malachi 1: 6 & 3: 10-12

The tither honors God by returning unto Him the holy portion. This woman was a tither, she was honoring God, and though there was no mention of her faith in her testimony, Jesus was still able to rescue her life and heal her body supernaturally, returning her to her husband and children, THROUGH THE OPEN DOOR OF HONOR!

Oh, hear me correctly believer. We must have faith in God. The Shunamite woman eventually developed her faith. When her son was grown, he was working in the fields and had a heat stroke and died. She lay her sons dead body in that upper chamber she had made for the man of God, and then rode off in haste to find Elisha. When asked by Gehazi

---

[15] (Thomas Nelson Publishers)

if anything was wrong with the child, she proclaimed, "It is well!" 2 Kings 4: 25-26

That tells me that she developed her faith. Developing your faith is vital. God expects you to have faith and to grow in faith, but it wasn't faith that made this woman a mother. It was her honor, and it was her honor that gave her an open door to have another audience with the prophet of God when the crisis of life came. I bet she was glad she hadn't grown familiar or offended with the prophet of God in the eighteen years or so since her son was born.

She honored, and stayed honorable, and over time she developed her faith. Her honor and her faith, were two powerful ingredients that when mixed with the anointing on the prophet, brought her dead son back to life!

Honor and faith. Faith and honor. We need both, for God is a faith God, and He rewards those who honor. Be sure you keep the switch of faith turned on in your life, but at the same time make sure that if Jesus can't reach your life any other way, that He'll be able to reach you through the open door of honor!

Chapter 7

Partnering with a Prophet

Philippians 1:3-4 (Passion NT) Emphasis Added

My prayers for you are full of praise to God as I give him thanks for you with great joy! ***I'm so grateful for our union*** [4] ***and our enduring partnership*** *that began the first time I presented to you the gospel.*[16]

In these last days, all of the five-fold ministry gifts will progress towards the fullness of their grace and anointing, including that of the prophet. Jesus is going to cause His prophets to rise up and take their place, while at the same time exposing all that is false and extreme.

As previously stated, the prophet's ministry is a valid and vital ministry, and as such, it is worthy of proper prayer support and funding. Should God desire it, you and I should be willing to tap into the power of partnership so that the one who carries the prophet's mantle can go all the places God calls him or her to go, and successfully reach all that God intends for them to reach. After all, what good is the voice of the prophet if no one ever hears it?

No minister will be able to fulfill their assignment alone. For every minister, including those who stand in the office of the prophet, God will supernaturally call others to stand along side to help, coming into a mutual partnership that will enable God's servant to fulfill their call. This was true for Jesus, and it was true for the Apostle Paul.

---

[16] (Simmons)

Here in Philippians, this great apostle and prophet is expressing his gratitude for the union and enduring partnership between he and them. They had a special bond together, a relationship birthed of the Spirit and spurred on by love.

Once and again, the Church at Philippi sent material aid to the Apostle Paul. Their care for him flourished again and again. They knew they could have a part in advancing the cause of Christ by faithfully supporting their spiritual father, and so they did.

The letter Paul wrote to the Philippians reveals two powerful benefits of spiritual partnership:

> ➢ His partners became partakers of his grace. Philippians 1: 7

> ➢ God would supply all their needs according to His riches in glory by Christ Jesus! Philippians 4: 19

What would it mean to become a partaker of someone else's grace? Well, it means that because you brought your supply to the man of God to help him further the call of God on his life, that you would become a one that receives of, benefits from, gains access to, the supernatural ability on that minister's life! Glory to God! What a benefit! It is the same principle we saw at work when Jesus said, "He who receives a prophet in the name of a prophet shall receive a prophet's reward." Matthew 10: 41

Because you are a partner with the prophet, you become a partaker of that prophet's anointing, a beneficiary if you will! No, you're not buying anything, but you are rewarded because of your love and enduring care for the one called to go and minister in places and to people you yourself could never reach. There is a reward bless God!

I'm a partner with a prophet. Why? Well, because God put us together first of all. Secondly, I love the man, and I am thrilled to have a small part in seeing him supplied and cared for. Thirdly, I believe in that prophet's anointing on his life. I know it will help others, and I can have a part in making sure they receive of the prophet's mantle by doing my part to send him. Fourth, through partnership I extend the reach of my life's fruitfulness beyond my own ability to go myself. The effect of my life's contribution, and therefore my eternal reward, is increased through the miracle of partnership! Lastly, I partner with the prophet that I might receive the prophet's reward!

Every member in the Body of Christ is called to help, and very often God will assign individual members of the Body of Christ to come into partnership with certain ministers and ministries for the advancement of the assignment on that ministry. We should never count that a light thing or ignore the Spirit of God's promptings. If He is dealing with us in this area, we should joyfully respond!

IS GOD CALLING YOU INTO PARTNERSHIP?

Is God calling you into partnership? If he is, act with confidence, like the Christians in Philippi, your life will be richly blessed when you obey!

Chapter 8

Meditations in Honor

In order for the Body of Christ to come into the fullness of what God has for us in this last day, and to experience the fullness of His presence, His glory, and the manifestations of His power, there must be a restoration of honor.

We who have the light on honor and its importance in the mind of God must do what we can to, by precept and example, teach the Body of Christ what we have learned.

I hope these statements on honor will stir you to reach for a higher standard in your life and ministry. The move of God for this era depends on it!

✓ *The Apostle Paul said, "I magnify my office." Romans 11: 13 Ministers should do all they can to carry their ministry office in honor, to make much of it, to not treat it as a light thing. We should conduct ourselves both in and out of the pulpit with the highest degree of dignity and integrity. Never denigrate your office of ministry, and don't let anyone else either.*

✓ *Eli put his sons before the Lord and dishonored himself as a Priest. In doing so, he lost his anointing, his place of service in the ministry, and both he and his sons lost their lives on the same day. Dishonor in ministry is a serious thing.*

✓ *Dress and honor are connected. You don't show up to a wedding in the same clothes you wear to Walmart because the occasion demands a higher standard. Standing before a blood bought people to preach under the anointing of God is an honor worthy of a higher level of dress than a wedding or any other occasion I can think of.*

✓ *It was over two years before I could be in the presence of my pastor without shaking. I was in such awe of how God was using him to change my life.*

✓ *I never allow my church members to address me by my first name, not because of ego, but because of honor. When they honor the office of the pastor on my life, it puts them in a position to receive.*

✓ *Honor is assigning the proper value to a person and treating them accordingly.*

✓ *There is a connection between honor and finances, whether you know it or not.*

✓ *It's dangerous to let yourself become familiar. The moment you do you'll never receive the same way again.*

✓ *As a minister, I will never design a service to be more pleasing and accommodating to people than to God.*

✓ *The more honor I bring to my man of God, the more I receive from him. The more honor I bring to my own office of ministry, the stronger the anointing becomes.*

✓ *I will forever be a student of honor.*

✓ *Honor shows up in our talk. It shows up in the words we use and our tone. Learn the language of honor.*

✓ *The failure to honor is costing us the miraculous. Dishonor disqualifies us from receiving from God.*

✓ *A failure to honor is a failure to recognize. The people of Nazareth didn't recognize the greatness of Jesus and they dishonored Him.*

✓ *Every human being is worthy of a degree of honor for the simple fact that they were created in the likeness and image of God.*

✓ *The local church will have to be the place where this generation learns and practices honor, for honor is absent in the home, the schools, the culture.*

✓ *What I know about honor I know because I was taught. People can't know what they are not taught.*

✓ *Honor is more than a virtue. It is a spiritual law.*

✓ *God's presence is drawn to honor. He does not manifest Himself, or His glory where He is not honored.*

✓ *What you fail to honor you will eventually lose.*

✓ *If you can't honor a man who you can see, how can you truly honor a God that you can't see?*

✓ *Honor will add years to your life. Dishonor will shorten your life.*

✓ *When in the presence of my spiritual parents, I give them their place as the teacher, and I take my place as the student.*

✓ *As a pastor, I honor my people by living prayerful, being well studied, and coming to my pulpit full of the Holy Ghost.*

Bibliography

American Dictionary of the English
Lanuage1828webstersdictionary1828.com

Holman Bible Publishers*Holy Bible, New King James Version*Nashville, TN U.S.A.Holman Bible Publishers1982

*KJV Dake Annotated Reference Bible*Lawrenceville, GA U.S.A.Dake Publishing2014

*The Exhaustive Concordinance of the Bible*Cicninnati, OH U.S.A.Jennings & Graham1890

*The Holy Bible, God's Word Translation*Ada, Michigan U.S.A.Baker Publishing Group1995

*The Passion Translation (TPT); with Psalms, Proverbs and Song of Songs*Savage, MN U.S.A.Broad Street Publishing2016

Thomas Nelson Publishers*Holy Bible, King James Version*Nashville, TN U.S.A.Thomas Nelson PublishersPublic Domain